The Presidents Bingo Book

COMPLETE BINGO GAME IN A BOOK

Portrait of George Washington by Gilbert Stuart

Written By Rebecca Stark

TITLE: Presidents Bingo
AUTHOR: Rebecca Stark

ISBN 978-0-87386-472-5

Educational Books 'n' Bingo

Printed in the U.S.A.

THE PRESIDENTS BINGO DIRECTIONS

INCLUDED:

List of Terms

Templates for Additional Terms and Clues

2 Clues per Term

30 Unique Bingo Cards

Markers

1. **Either cut apart the book or make copies of ALL the sheets. You might want to make an extra copy of the clue sheets to use for introduction and review. Keep the sheets in an envelope for easy reuse.**

2. Cut apart the call cards with terms and clues.

3. Pass out one bingo card per student. There are enough for a class of 30.

4. Pass out markers. You may cut apart the markers included in this book or use any other small items of your choice.

5. Decide whether or not you will require the entire card to be filled. Requiring the entire card to be filled provides a better review. However, if you have a short time to fill, you may prefer to have them do the just the border or some other format. Tell the class before you begin what is required.

6. There are 50 terms. Read the list before you begin. If there are any terms that have not been covered in class, you may want to read to the students the term and clues before you begin.

7. There is a blank space in the middle of each card. You can instruct the students to use it as a free space or you can write in answers to cover terms not included. Of course, in this case you would create your own clues. (Templates provided.)

8. Shuffle the cards and place them in a pile. Two or three clues are provided for each term. If you plan to play the game with the same group more than once, you might want to choose a different clue for each game. If not, you may choose to use more than one clue.

9. Be sure to keep the cards you have used for the present game in a separate pile. When a student calls, "Bingo," he or she will have to verify that the correct answers are on his or her card AND that the markers were placed in response to the proper questions. Pull out the cards that are on the student's card keeping them in the order they were used in the game. Read each clue as it was given and ask the student to identify the correct answer from his or her card.

10. If the student has the correct answers on the card AND has shown that they were marked in response to the *correct questions,* then that student is the winner and the game is over. If the student does not have the correct answers on the card OR he or she marked the answers in response to *the wrong questions,* then the game continues until there is a proper winner.

11. If you want to play again, reshuffle the cards and begin again.

Have fun!

PEOPLE FEATURED

PRESIDENTS

GEORGE WASHINGTON

JOHN ADAMS

JEFFERSON

JAMES MADISON

JAMES MONROE

JOHN QUINCY ADAMS

ANDREW JACKSON

MARTIN VAN BUREN

WILLIAM HENRY HARRISON

JOHN TYLER

JAMES KNOX POLK

ZACHARY TAYLOR

MILLARD FILLMORE

FRANKLIN PIERCE

JAMES BUCHANAN

ABRAHAM LINCOLN

ANDREW JOHNSON

ULYSSES SIMPSON GRANT

RUTHERFORD BIRCHARD HAYES

JAMES ABRAM GARFIELD

CHESTER ALAN ARTHUR

GROVER CLEVELAND

BENJAMIN HARRISON

GROVER CLEVELAND

WILLIAM MCKINLEY

THEODORE ROOSEVELT

WILLIAM HOWARD TAFT

WOODROW WILSON

WARREN GAMALIEL HARDING

CALVIN COOLIDGE

HERBERT CLARK HOOVER

FRANKLIN DELANO ROOSEVELT

HARRY S. TRUMAN

DWIGHT DAVID EISENHOWER

JOHN FITZGERALD KENNEDY

LYNDON BAINES JOHNSON

RICHARD MILHOUS NIXON

GERALD RUDOLPH FORD

JAMES EARL CARTER, JR.

RONALD WILSON REAGAN

GEORGE HERBERT WALKER BUSH

WILLIAM JEFFERSON CLINTON

GEORGE WALKER BUSH

BARACK OBAMA

DONALD J. TRUMP

JOSEPH ROBINETTE (JOE) BIDEN, JR.

A FEW FIRST LADIES

MARTHA WASHINGTON

DOLLEY MADISON

(ANNA) ELEANOR ROOSEVELT

JACQUELINE KENNEDY

HILLARY RODHAM CLINTON

Additional Terms

Choose as many additional terms as you would like and write them in the squares. Repeat each as desired.
Cut out the squares and randomly distribute them to the class.
Instruct the students to place their square on the center space of their card.

Clues for Additional Terms

Write three clues for each of your additional terms.

1.

2.

3.

1.

2.

3.

1.

2.

3.

1.

2.

3.

1.

2.

3.

1.

2.

3.

George Washington	**John Adams**
1. The first President of the United States, he ruled from 1780 to 1797.	1. The second President of the United States, he ruled from 1797 to 1801.
2. He was elected Commander in Chief of the Continental Army by the Second Continental Congress.	2. He and Jefferson were the only two Presidents to have signed the Declaration of Independence.
3. Mount Vernon, located near Alexandria, Virginia, was the name of his plantation home.	3. This Harvard-educated lawyer from Massachusetts was a member of both the First and the Second Continental Congresses.
Jefferson	**James Madison**
1. The third President of the United States, he ruled from 1801 to 1809.	1. The fourth President of the United States, he ruled from 1809 to 1817.
2. He drafted the *Declaration of Independence.*	2. He is known as the "Father of the U.S. Constitution."
3. He was President at the time of the Louisiana Purchase.	3. He asked Congress to declare war on Great Britain on June 1, 1812, because of the British impressment of American seamen and the seizure of cargoes.
James Monroe	**John Quincy Adams**
1. The fifth President of the United States, he ruled from 1817 to 1825.	1. The sixth President of the United States, he ruled from 1825 to 1829.
2. Spain ceded Florida to the United States and the *Missouri Compromise* admitted Missouri as a slave state during his presidency.	2. He was the first President who was the son of a President.
3. John Quincy Adams helped him formulate his doctrine of noncolonization and nonintervention by Europe.	3. As Secretary of State under President Monroe, he was instrumental in obtaining the cession of the Floridas from Spain and he helped formulate the Monroe Doctrine.
Andrew Jackson	**Martin Van Buren**
1. The seventh President of the United States, he ruled from 1829 to 1837.	1. The eighth President of the United States, he ruled from 1837 to 1841.
2. His nickname was "Old Hickory."	2. He was President during the Panic of 1837, the nation's first true depression.
3. He rewarded many of his political supporters with government jobs. His critics provided a name for this practice, calling it the "spoils system."	3. He lost his bid for reelection, partly because of his refusal to annex Texas.
William Henry Harrison	**John Tyler**
1. The ninth President of the United States, he ruled in 1841.	1. The tenth President of the United States, he ruled from 1841 to 1845.
2. He fought against Native Americans at the Battle of Tippecanoe in 1811, where he earned the nickname "Tippecanoe."	2. He became President when William Henry Harrison died after only one month in office.
3. He died one month after taking office. It was the briefest presidency in U.S. history.	3. His opponents nicknamed him "His Accidency" due to the way in which he assumed office.

Presidents Bingo

James Knox Polk 1. The eleventh President of the United States, he ruled from 1845 to 1849. 2. He was President during the Mexican–American War. 3. Like other Jacksonian Democrats, he was committed to Manifest Destiny and through the Treaty of Guadalupe Hidalgo, he secured the Oregon Territory.	**Zachary Taylor** 1. The twelfth President of the United States, he ruled from 1849 to 1850. 2. He was nicknamed "Old Rough and Ready." 3. He served only 16 months before dying in office. He was the second President to die in office.
Millard Fillmore 1. The thirteenth President of the United States, he ruled from 1850 to 1853. 2. As a youth he worked on his father's farm, and at 15 was apprenticed to a cloth dresser. 3. He became President when Zachary Taylor died. He appointed Daniel Webster Secretary of State.	**Franklin Pierce** 1. The fourteenth President of the United States, he ruled from 1853 to 1857. 2. He endorsed the Kansas-Nebraska Bill, which allowed settlers there to decide whether or not to permit slavery, angering his fellow Northerners. 3. Jefferson Davis, who later served as President of the Confederacy, was Secretary of War under this President.
James Buchanan 1. The fifteenth President of the United States, he ruled from 1857 to 1861. 2. The Dred Scott Decision was made during his Presidency. 3. When 7 states seceded, he said they had no legal right to secede but held that the Federal Government legally could not prevent them.	**Abraham Lincoln** 1. The sixteenth President of the United States, he ruled from 1861 to 1865. 2. He issued the Emancipation Proclamation. 3. He was President during the American Civil War.
Andrew Johnson 1. The seventeenth President of the United States, he ruled from 1865 to 1869. 2. He became President when President Lincoln was assassinated. 3. He was impeached because of his handling of Reconstruction but was acquitted.	**Ulysses Simpson Grant** 1. The eighteenth President of the United States, he ruled from 1869 to 1877. 2. He was General in Chief of all Federal Armies during the American Civil War. 3. The fifteenth amendment, which gave all qualified male citizens the right to vote, was passed during his administration.
Rutherford Birchard Hayes 1. The nineteenth President of the United States, he ruled from 1877 to 1881. 2. Although his opponent, Governor Tilden of New York, received about 260,000 more popular votes, he won the election by 1 electoral vote. 3. He invited Edison to the White House to demonstrate his new tin-foil phonograph in April 1878.	**James Abram Garfield** 1. Twentieth President of the United States, he ruled in 1881. 2. Clara Barton organized the American Association of the Red Cross on May 21, 1881, during his short presidency. 3. He was shot on July 2, 1881, by Charles Guiteau, who had wanted a consular post and did not get it; he died a few months later.

Presidents Bingo

© Barbara M. Peller

Chester Alan Arthur 1. Twenty-first President of the United States, he ruled from 1881 to 1885. 2. During his administration Congress passed the Pendleton Act, which established the Civil Service Commission and put and end to the so-called "spoils system." 3. He is sometimes called the "Father of Civil Service."	**Grover Cleveland** 1. As the twenty-second and twenty-fourth President of the United States, he ruled from 1885 to 1889 and from 1893 to 1897. 2. He is the only President to have served two nonconsecutive terms. 3. He signed the Interstate Commerce Act of 1887, the first law attempting federal regulation of the railroads.
Benjamin Harrison 1. Twenty-third President of the United States, he ruled from 1889 to 1893. 2. His grandfather, the ninth President, was nicknamed "Old Tippecanoe." 3. He signed the Sherman Anti-Trust Act, the first federal act attempting to prevent monopolies.	**William McKinley** 1. The twenty-fifth President of the United States, he ruled from 1897 to 1901. 2. The Spanish-American War took place during his administration; it was precipitated by the sinking of the *Maine* in Havana Harbor. 3. He was shot by an anarchist while at the Pan-American Exposition in Buffalo, New York. He died about a week later.
Theodore Roosevelt 1. This twenty-sixth President of the United States ruled from 1901 to 1909. 2. As a lieutenant colonel of the Rough Riders, he was a hero of the Spanish-American War. 3. He permanently preserved about 230,000,000 acres of land as national parks and forests, game and bird preserves, and other federal reservations.	**William Howard Taft** 1. The twenty-seventh President of the United States, he ruled from 1909 to 1913. 2. President Harding made him Chief Justice of the United States, a position he held until just before his death in 1930. 3. Arizona was admitted as the 48th state during his administration.
Woodrow Wilson 1. This twenty-eighth President of the United States ruled from 1913 to 1921. 2. He asked Congress to declare war on Germany and said America's entrance into World War I was a crusade to make the world "safe for democracy." 3. The Federal Reserve System, the central banking system of the United States, was created during his administration.	**Warren Gamaliel Harding** 1. This twenty-ninth President of the United States ruled from 1921 to 1923. 2. In July of 1921 he signed a joint congressional resolution declaring the official end of war with Germany. 3. News of the Teapot Dome Scandal began to break shortly before his death.
Calvin Coolidge 1. This thirtieth President of the United States ruled from 1923 to 1929. 2. He restored public confidence in the White House after the scandals of the Harding Administration. 3. He signed the Immigration Act of 1924, which limited the number of immigrants who could be admitted to the United States.	**Herbert Clark Hoover** 1. Thirty-first President of the United States, he ruled from 1929 to 1933. 2. The Great Depression began during his administration with the stock market crash of 1929. 3. The dam in the Black Canyon of the Colorado River on the border between Arizona and Nevada was built during his administration and is named after him.

Presidents Bingo

Franklin Delano Roosevelt	**Harry S. Truman**
1. Thirty-second President of the United States, he ruled from 1933 to 1945. 2. He was President when the Japanese attacked Pearl Harbor on December 7, 1941. 3. He is and always will be the only President ever to be elected for four terms.	1. The thirty-third President of the United States, he ruled from 1945 to 1953. 2. He ordered atomic bombs to be dropped on Hiroshima and Nagasaki. Japanese surrender followed. 3. The United Nations and NATO were established during his administration.
Dwight David Eisenhower	**John Fitzgerald Kennedy**
1. The thirty-fourth President of the United States, he ruled from 1953 to 1961. 2. He had been commanding general of the victorious forces in Europe during World War II. 3. During his administration the Supreme Court ruled in *Brown v. Topeka Board of Education* that racial segregation in public schools is unconstitutional.	1. The thirty-fifth President of the United States, he ruled from 1961 to 1963. 2. His book *Profiles in Courage* won the Pulitzer Prize in history. 3. During his presidency Yuri Gagarin became the 1st person in space; Alan Sheppard, Jr,. the 1st American in space; and John Glenn the 1st American to orbit Earth.
Lyndon Baines Johnson	**Richard Milhous Nixon**
1. Thirty-sixth President of the United States, he ruled from 1963 to 1969. 2. He became President when President Kennedy was assassinated. 3. The Civil Rights Act of 1964 was passed during his administration.	1. Thirty-seventh President of the United States, he ruled from 1969 to 1974. 2. During his administration the Paris Peace Accords were signed, ending the the Vietnam War. The U.S. was involved in that war from 1965 to 1973. 3. Faced with the likelihood of impeachment due to the Watergate scandal, he resigned.
Gerald Rudolph Ford	**James Earl Carter, Jr.**
1. Thirty-eighth President of the United States, he ruled from 1974 to 1977. 2. He became Vice President when Spiro Agnew resigned because of criminal charges. 3. He was the first to succeed a resigning President. He later pardoned that President.	1. The thirty-ninth President of the United States, he ruled from 1977 to 1981. 2. He was a peanut farmer from Plains, Georgia. 3. Through the Camp David agreement of 1978 he helped bring peace between Egypt and Israel.
Ronald Wilson Reagan	**George Herbert Walker Bush**
1. This fortieth President of the United States ruled from 1981 to 1989. 2. The Iran-Contra Affair, involving trading arms for hostages, took place during his administration. 3. He helped to accelerate an end to the Cold War. In 1986 he and Gorbachev met at Reykjavik, Iceland, for a summit at which they discussed eliminating all nuclear weapons.	1. Forty-first President of the United States, he ruled from 1989 to 1993. 2. The Berlin Wall fell during his administration, marking the symbolic end of Communist rule in Eastern Europe. 3. He was President during the Persian Gulf War, code-named Operation Desert Storm.

Presidents Bingo

William Jefferson Clinton 1. Forty-second President of the United States, he ruled from 1993 to 2001. 2. He was the 2nd U.S. president to be impeached by the House of Representatives. He was tried in the Senate and found not guilty. 3. The North American Free Trade Agreement, or NAFTA, is a trade bloc created by the U.S., Canada, & Mexico during his administration.	**George Walker Bush** 1. This forty-third President of the United States ruled from 2001 to 2009. 2. He was President when the terrorist attack on the World Trade Center in New York on September 11, 2001, occurred. 3. The Iraq War began in 2003 under his leadership.
Barack Obama 1. Forty-fourth President of the United States, his 8 years in office began in 2009. 2. He was the first African American President of the United States. 3 He was a member of the Illinois Senate from 1996 until 2004, when he was elected to the United States Senate.	**Donald J. Trump** 1. He was the 45th and 47th Prseident. 2. Until he became President, he was best known as a real-estate developer and a tv reality-show host. 3. He was impeached twice.
Joseph (Joe) Robinette Biden, Jr. 1. He served as the 47th vice president during the Obama administration. 2. He was a United States Senator from Delaware for 36 years: from January 3, 1973, to January 15, 2009. 3. His vice president, Kamala Harris, was the first female to hold that position.	**Martha Washington** 1. She was the first first lady of the United States. 2. She lived at the President's House in the two temporary capitals, New York and Philadelphia. 3. She is buried near her husband at Mount Vernon.
Dolley Madison 1. Her home was the center of society during the years her husband was Secretary of State under Jefferson, who was a widower. 2. In 1809 she presided at the 1st inaugural ball in Washington when her husband became President. 3. When forced to flee the White House because of a British attack during the War of 1812, she saved some papers and a portrait of George Washington.	**(Anna) Eleanor Roosevelt** 1. She transformed the role of first lady by holding press conferences, traveling throughout the country, and giving lectures & radio broadcasts. 2. She expressed her opinions in a syndicated newspaper column entitled "My Day." 3. She resigned from the Daughters of the American Revolution because they refused to let Marian Anderson sing at Constitution Hall.
Jacqueline Kennedy 1. She was with her husband when he was assassinated in Dallas. 2. From 1978 until her death in 1994, she worked in New York City as an editor for Doubleday. 3. She became the most prominent proponent for the establishment of the National Cultural Center in Washington, DC; it was eventually named for her husband.	**Hillary Rodham Clinton** 1. She was the first female to be nominated for President by a major politcal party. 2. This former first lady was the first female U.S. senator to represent New York. 3. She was Secretary of State under President Obama from 2009 to 2013.

Presidents Bingo

The Presidents Bingo

George H. W. Bush	George Washington	John Quincy Adams	Theodore Roosevelt	Benjamin Harrison
Ronald Reagan	Hillary Rodham Clinton	George W. Bush	Calvin Coolidge	Martha Washington
James Madison	Jacqueline (Jackie) Kennedy		Thomas Jefferson	Andrew Johnson
James (Jimmy) Carter	Zachary Taylor	Joseph (Joe) R. Biden, Jr.	Woodrow Wilson	Franklin Delano Roosevelt
Dwight David Eisenhower	Ulysses S. Grant	William McKinley	Barack Obama	William (Bill) Clinton

The Presidents Bingo

James (Jimmy) Carter	James Madison	Dolley Madison	(Anna) Eleanor Roosevelt	Chester A. Arthur
Franklin Delano Roosevelt	John Tyler	John Adams	Zachary Taylor	Gerald Ford
Martin Van Buren	Ulysses S. Grant		James Buchanan	Joseph (Joe) R. Biden, Jr.
Donald J. Trump	Richard Nixon	Jacqueline (Jackie) Kennedy	Lyndon Baines Johnson	William (Bill) Clinton
Martha Washington	George W. Bush	William McKinley	Hillary Rodham Clinton	Barack Obama

The Presidents Bingo

James (Jimmy) Carter	Joseph (Joe) R. Biden, Jr.	John Tyler	Woodrow Wilson	James Madison
Calvin Coolidge	Thomas Jefferson	William Henry Harrison	George Washington	William Howard Taft
Zachary Taylor	George W. Bush		Gerald Ford	James Monroe
Jacqueline (Jackie) Kennedy	Martin Van Buren	Dwight David Eisenhower	Donald J. Trump	Dolley Madison
Barack Obama	Hillary Rodham Clinton	William McKinley	Lyndon Baines Johnson	Chester A. Arthur

The Presidents Bingo

Jacqueline (Jackie) Kennedy	William (Bill) Clinton	John Quincy Adams	Hillary Rodham Clinton	Chester A. Arthur
Warren G. Harding	Andrew Jackson	George Washington	(Anna) Eleanor Roosevelt	James Madison
Thomas Jefferson	Donald J. Trump		Benjamin Harrison	Theodore Roosevelt
Joseph (Joe) R. Biden, Jr.	Millard Fillmore	George W. Bush	William McKinley	John Adams
Grover Cleveland	Martha Washington	Harry S. Truman	Barack Obama	Andrew Johnson

The Presidents Bingo

Martha Washington	Benjamin Harrison	Barack Obama	John Adams	Hillary Rodham Clinton
Warren G. Harding	Joseph (Joe) R. Biden, Jr.	William Henry Harrison	James Buchanan	Thomas Jefferson
John Quincy Adams	Andrew Johnson		Calvin Coolidge	Rutherford B. Hayes
William (Bill) Clinton	Chester A. Arthur	George H. W. Bush	Lyndon Baines Johnson	James Knox Polk
John Tyler	William McKinley	James Madison	Jacqueline (Jackie) Kennedy	Grover Cleveland

Presidents Bingo: Card No. 5

© Barbara M. Peller

The Presidents Bingo

James Monroe	Joseph (Joe) R. Biden, Jr.	Dolley Madison	Chester A. Arthur	Andrew Johnson
Woodrow Wilson	Zachary Taylor	James Knox Polk	George Washington	James Madison
(Anna) Eleanor Roosevelt	Abraham Lincoln		Andrew Jackson	James Buchanan
William McKinley	Dwight David Eisenhower	Lyndon Baines Johnson	Harry S. Truman	John Quincy Adams
Franklin Delano Roosevelt	John Adams	Grover Cleveland	George H. W. Bush	Millard Fillmore

The Presidents Bingo

Grover Cleveland	Gerald Ford	Rutherford B. Hayes	Calvin Coolidge	John Tyler
Franklin Delano Roosevelt	Chester A. Arthur	Ulysses S. Grant	Thomas Jefferson	Warren G. Harding
Dolley Madison	Theodore Roosevelt		James Buchanan	Andrew Jackson
Jacqueline (Jackie) Kennedy	Donald J. Trump	William Henry Harrison	James (Jimmy) Carter	Martin Van Buren
William McKinley	Hillary Rodham Clinton	Lyndon Baines Johnson	Harry S. Truman	James Monroe

The Presidents Bingo

George H. W. Bush	Gerald Ford	Franklin Pierce	Woodrow Wilson	Andrew Jackson
Warren G. Harding	John Quincy Adams	(Anna) Eleanor Roosevelt	Andrew Johnson	John Adams
Millard Fillmore	John Fitzgerald Kennedy		Chester A. Arthur	Benjamin Harrison
Barack Obama	Jacqueline (Jackie) Kennedy	James (Jimmy) Carter	Abraham Lincoln	Donald J. Trump
George W. Bush	William McKinley	Harry S. Truman	Zachary Taylor	Franklin Delano Roosevelt

The Presidents Bingo

James Buchanan	John Tyler	Ulysses S. Grant	Millard Fillmore	Hillary Rodham Clinton
Abraham Lincoln	Chester A. Arthur	Thomas Jefferson	Zachary Taylor	Gerald Ford
William Howard Taft	George H. W. Bush		Grover Cleveland	Franklin Pierce
James Knox Polk	William (Bill) Clinton	Dwight David Eisenhower	Calvin Coolidge	Rutherford B. Hayes
Donald J. Trump	Lyndon Baines Johnson	William Henry Harrison	James (Jimmy) Carter	Benjamin Harrison

The Presidents Bingo

James (Jimmy) Carter	Woodrow Wilson	Andrew Jackson	(Anna) Eleanor Roosevelt	Millard Fillmore
Andrew Johnson	John Adams	George Washington	Thomas Jefferson	Chester A. Arthur
John Fitzgerald Kennedy	William (Bill) Clinton		Theodore Roosevelt	Martin Van Buren
Dwight David Eisenhower	Gerald Ford	James Knox Polk	Lyndon Baines Johnson	William Howard Taft
William Henry Harrison	Franklin Delano Roosevelt	Dolley Madison	Martha Washington	Grover Cleveland

The Presidents Bingo

James Monroe	Gerald Ford	Zachary Taylor	James Knox Polk	Franklin Delano Roosevelt
Franklin Pierce	William Howard Taft	Calvin Coolidge	James Buchanan	George Washington
Warren G. Harding	Chester A. Arthur		Dolley Madison	Ulysses S. Grant
William Henry Harrison	James Madison	Lyndon Baines Johnson	Hillary Rodham Clinton	James (Jimmy) Carter
Abraham Lincoln	William McKinley	Grover Cleveland	Harry S. Truman	John Tyler

The Presidents Bingo

John Tyler	Benjamin Harrison	William Howard Taft	Woodrow Wilson	James Buchanan
Ulysses S. Grant	Franklin Delano Roosevelt	John Quincy Adams	Harry S. Truman	Thomas Jefferson
George H. W. Bush	Rutherford B. Hayes		Andrew Johnson	(Anna) Eleanor Roosevelt
William McKinley	Donald J. Trump	Chester A. Arthur	James (Jimmy) Carter	Warren G. Harding
Gerald Ford	Franklin Pierce	John Fitzgerald Kennedy	Abraham Lincoln	John Adams

Presidents Bingo: Card No. 12

The Presidents Bingo

James Knox Polk	Benjamin Harrison	James Monroe	William Howard Taft	Andrew Johnson
John Quincy Adams	Franklin Pierce	Chester A. Arthur	James Buchanan	Martin Van Buren
Woodrow Wilson	John Tyler		Ulysses S. Grant	Rutherford B. Hayes
Thomas Jefferson	Lyndon Baines Johnson	Andrew Jackson	John Fitzgerald Kennedy	James (Jimmy) Carter
William McKinley	William (Bill) Clinton	Harry S. Truman	Grover Cleveland	Calvin Coolidge

The Presidents Bingo

Hillary Rodham Clinton	Chester A. Arthur	Zachary Taylor	James Buchanan	Abraham Lincoln
John Adams	Grover Cleveland	William Howard Taft	Thomas Jefferson	William (Bill) Clinton
John Knox Polk	Theodore Roosevelt		Dolley Madison	William Henry Harrison
Gerald Ford	Lyndon Baines Johnson	John Fitzgerald Kennedy	Andrew Jackson	James Monroe
William McKinley	(Anna) Eleanor Roosevelt	Martin Van Buren	Franklin Delano Roosevelt	George H. W. Bush

The Presidents Bingo

Calvin Coolidge	James Buchanan	Zachary Taylor	John Tyler	Woodrow Wilson
James Monroe	Dolley Madison	George Washington	John Quincy Adams	Abraham Lincoln
Andrew Johnson	George H. W. Bush		James Madison	Gerald Ford
William McKinley	William Howard Taft	Franklin Pierce	Lyndon Baines Johnson	John Knox Polk
Franklin Delano Roosevelt	Donald J. Trump	Harry S. Truman	Millard Fillmore	Ulysses S. Grant

The Presidents Bingo

Andrew Jackson	William Howard Taft	Franklin Pierce	Millard Fillmore	Lyndon Baines Johnson
(Anna) Eleanor Roosevelt	Martin Van Buren	Rutherford B. Hayes	Warren G. Harding	Theodore Roosevelt
James Knox Polk	Benjamin Harrison		Andrew Johnson	Ulysses S. Grant
Jacqueline (Jackie) Kennedy	John Adams	William McKinley	Herbert C. Hoover	James (Jimmy) Carter
Abraham Lincoln	George H. W. Bush	Harry S. Truman	Donald J. Trump	Gerald Ford

The Presidents Bingo

William Henry Harrison	Herbert C. Hoover	James A. Garfield	William Howard Taft	Hillary Rodham Clinton
Calvin Coolidge	Abraham Lincoln	Lyndon Baines Johnson	Theodore Roosevelt	Rutherford B. Hayes
James Buchanan	Thomas Jefferson		George H. W. Bush	Franklin Pierce
Gerald Ford	Franklin Delano Roosevelt	James (Jimmy) Carter	Zachary Taylor	Martin Van Buren
Dwight David Eisenhower	James Knox Polk	John Tyler	Woodrow Wilson	Benjamin Harrison

The Presidents Bingo

Millard Fillmore	John Fitzgerald Kennedy	John Adams	James Knox Polk	(Anna) Eleanor Roosevelt
William (Bill) Clinton	William Henry Harrison	Dwight David Eisenhower	Andrew Johnson	Abraham Lincoln
James Buchanan	Martin Van Buren		James A. Garfield	John Quincy Adams
Gerald Ford	George Washington	Lyndon Baines Johnson	James (Jimmy) Carter	Dolley Madison
Ronald Reagan	William Howard Taft	Zachary Taylor	Herbert C. Hoover	James Monroe

The Presidents Bingo

Andrew Johnson	James Monroe	William Howard Taft	Franklin Pierce	George Washington
Calvin Coolidge	Woodrow Wilson	Gerald Ford	John Tyler	Theodore Roosevelt
Herbert C. Hoover	Hillary Rodham Clinton		Thomas Jefferson	James Madison
Dolley Madison	Ronald Reagan	Dwight David Eisenhower	Donald J. Trump	James A. Garfield
John Quincy Adams	Richard Nixon	Franklin Delano Roosevelt	George H. W. Bush	Harry S. Truman

The Presidents Bingo

John Fitzgerald Kennedy	Herbert C. Hoover	Woodrow Wilson	William Howard Taft	Harry S. Truman
John Adams	Ulysses S. Grant	Warren G. Harding	Dwight David Eisenhower	(Anna) Eleanor Roosevelt
Benjamin Harrison	Rutherford B. Hayes		Jacqueline (Jackie) Kennedy	George Washington
Martha Washington	George W. Bush	Barack Obama	Donald J. Trump	Ronald Reagan
Joseph (Joe) R. Biden, Jr.	Hillary Rodham Clinton	Richard Nixon	James (Jimmy) Carter	James A. Garfield

The Presidents Bingo

Calvin Coolidge	James Monroe	Warren G. Harding	William Howard Taft	Martha Washington
Benjamin Harrison	James A. Garfield	Andrew Jackson	Franklin Pierce	George H. W. Bush
Martin Van Buren	Franklin Delano Roosevelt		Herbert C. Hoover	Zachary Taylor
Dwight David Eisenhower	John Tyler	John Adams	Grover Cleveland	Ronald Reagan
Jacqueline (Jackie) Kennedy	Richard Nixon	Harry S. Truman	William Henry Harrison	Donald J. Trump

The Presidents Bingo

Millard Fillmore	Dolley Madison	James A. Garfield	John Quincy Adams	John Knox Polk
(Anna) Eleanor Roosevelt	Woodrow Wilson	James Madison	Franklin Pierce	Thomas Jefferson
John Adams	Theodore Roosevelt		Grover Cleveland	Rutherford B. Hayes
Ronald Reagan	Gerald Ford	Donald J. Trump	George Washington	Hillary Rodham Clinton
Richard Nixon	William Henry Harrison	Herbert C. Hoover	Martin Van Buren	Warren G. Harding

Presidents Bingo

Andrew Jackson	Herbert C. Hoover	John Tyler	John Quincy Adams	Harry S. Truman
James Monroe	John Fitzgerald Kennedy	Franklin Delano Roosevelt	Calvin Coolidge	George Washington
Dolley Madison	James Knox Polk		Barack Obama	Grover Cleveland
Martin Van Buren	Richard Nixon	James Madison	William Henry Harrison	Donald J. Trump
Martha Washington	George W. Bush	Ulysses S. Grant	Dwight David Eisenhower	James A. Garfield

The Presidents Bingo

George Washington	John Fitzgerald Kennedy	Hillary Rodham Clinton	Herbert C. Hoover	Grover Cleveland
James A. Garfield	George W. Bush	Warren G. Harding	(Anna) Eleanor Roosevelt	George H. W. Bush
Dwight David Eisenhower	Millard Fillmore		James Knox Polk	Martin Van Buren
Martha Washington	Barack Obama	Ronald Reagan	Donald J. Trump	Benjamin Harrison
Joseph (Joe) R. Biden, Jr.	Jacqueline (Jackie) Kennedy	Richard Nixon	Woodrow Wilson	Harry S. Truman

The Presidents Bingo

Jacqueline (Jackie) Kennedy	Warren G. Harding	Herbert C. Hoover	Zachary Taylor	James A. Garfield
George Washington	William (Bill) Clinton	Calvin Coolidge	Andrew Jackson	Thomas Jefferson
Benjamin Harrison	Franklin Pierce		Barack Obama	Ronald Reagan
James Madison	Martha Washington	George W. Bush	Richard Nixon	Theodore Roosevelt
Harry S. Truman	Hillary Rodham Clinton	John Adams	Abraham Lincoln	Joseph (Joe) R. Biden, Jr.

The Presidents Bingo

James A. Garfield	Herbert C. Hoover	Dolley Madison	(Anna) Eleanor Roosevelt	Millard Fillmore
Dwight David Eisenhower	Woodrow Wilson	Franklin Pierce	John Fitzgerald Kennedy	Andrew Jackson
William (Bill) Clinton	Barack Obama		Theodore Roosevelt	Jacqueline (Jackie) Kennedy
William Henry Harrison	John Quincy Adams	Martha Washington	Richard Nixon	Ronald Reagan
Rutherford B. Hayes	Abraham Lincoln	Zachary Taylor	George W. Bush	Joseph (Joe) R. Biden, Jr.

The Presidents Bingo

Dolley Madison	John Adams	Herbert C. Hoover	John Fitzgerald Kennedy	Ulysses S. Grant
Martha Washington	Barack Obama	Calvin Coolidge	Ronald Reagan	Thomas Jefferson
Lyndon Baines Johnson	George W. Bush		Richard Nixon	Jacqueline (Jackie) Kennedy
Millard Fillmore	James Monroe	Warren G. Harding	Joseph (Joe) R. Biden, Jr.	George Washington
Abraham Lincoln	Theodore Roosevelt	James A. Garfield	James Madison	Rutherford B. Hayes

The Presidents Bingo

Andrew Johnson	John Fitzgerald Kennedy	James Madison	Herbert C. Hoover	Andrew Jackson
Ulysses S. Grant	James A. Garfield	Barack Obama	(Anna) Eleanor Roosevelt	Theodore Roosevelt
George W. Bush	Martin Van Buren		Rutherford B. Hayes	Dwight David Eisenhower
James (Jimmy) Carter	Millard Fillmore	Franklin Delano Roosevelt	Richard Nixon	Ronald Reagan
John Quincy Adams	Grover Cleveland	George H. W. Bush	Joseph (Joe) R. Biden, Jr.	Martha Washington

The Presidents Bingo

James A. Garfield	John Fitzgerald Kennedy	Millard Fillmore	Calvin Coolidge	George H. W. Bush
Hillary Rodham Clinton	Dwight David Eisenhower	Warren G. Harding	Rutherford B. Hayes	James Madison
Benjamin Harrison	Barack Obama		Thomas Jefferson	Herbert C. Hoover
Ulysses S. Grant	Martha Washington	Chester A. Arthur	Richard Nixon	Ronald Reagan
Andrew Jackson	Franklin Pierce	Joseph (Joe) R. Biden, Jr.	James Monroe	George W. Bush

The Presidents Bingo

Grover Cleveland	Herbert C. Hoover	(Anna) Eleanor Roosevelt	George H. W. Bush	Ronald Reagan
George Washington	John Fitzgerald Kennedy	Dolley Madison	Theodore Roosevelt	Thomas Jefferson
Gerald Ford	William (Bill) Clinton		Rutherford B. Hayes	Warren G. Harding
Joseph (Joe) R. Biden, Jr.	James Monroe	John Quincy Adams	Richard Nixon	Barack Obama
Martha Washington	John Tyler	George W. Bush	James A. Garfield	James Madison